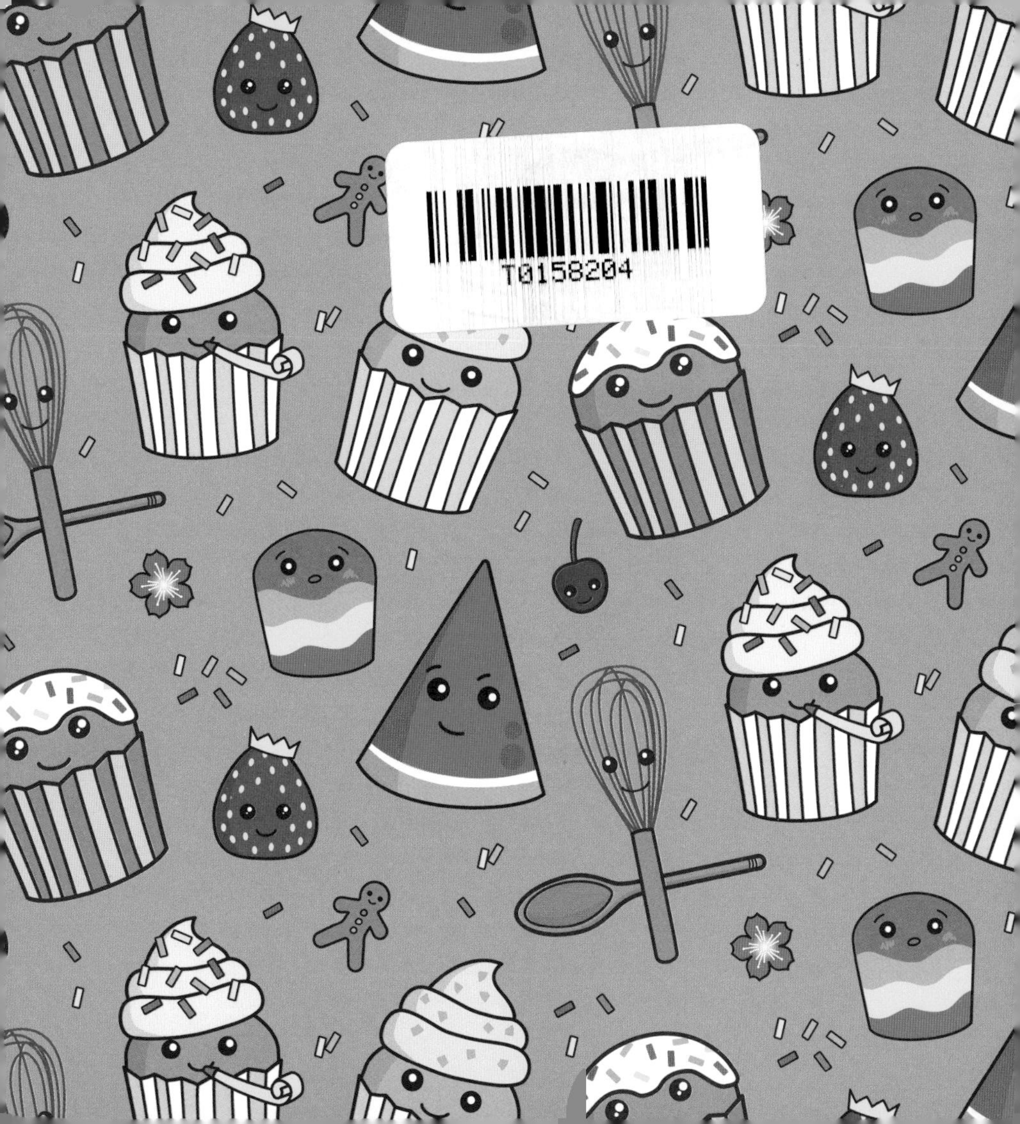

Published by Ice House Books

Copyright © 2020 Cakes with Faces
Licensed by This is Iris. www.thisisiris.co.uk

Written & illustrated by Cakes With Faces creator, Amy Crabtree

Ice House Books is an imprint of Half Moon Bay Limited
The Ice House, 124 Walcot Street, Bath, BA1 5BG
www.icehousebooks.co.uk

ISBN 978-1-912867-71-4

Printed in China

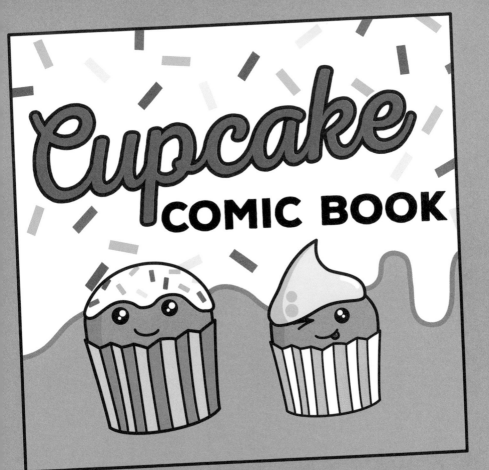

Cupcake
COMIC BOOK

ICE HOUSE BOOKS

ABOUT
CAKES WITH FACES

1) Cakes with Faces designs are all original art by UK designer Amy Crabtree.

2) I love drawing cute designs to make you smile, and to make every day more fun.

3) It started as a hobby, and now it's my full time job. I design t-shirts, clothing and gifts. You can see them on cakeswithfaces.co.uk

4) I love travelling to Japan, and making travel videos on YouTube. It's also a big inspiration for my artwork.

CAKESWITHFACES.CO.UK

WHERE TO GET SUPPLIES

CAKE DECORATING SHOPS
Look for your local cake-decorating shop to browse what's on offer. The staff might be able to help with advice and recommendations.

ONLINE
If you can't find what you need in a local shop, you can order almost anything online! Especially for specific or unusual items, like flavourings and magical sprinkles – you'll have the biggest choice.

CRAFT SUPERSTORES
Large arts and crafts stores sometimes have a cake-decorating section with tempting tools and gadgets.

SUPERMARKETS
There's often a small cake-decorating section with cases, colouring and basic decorations. Good for last minute emergencies if you've forgotten anything! And you can pick up your baking ingredients too.

NATURAL FOOD COLOURING

If you want colourful icing but don't like the idea of all the e-numbers and mystery ingredients in artifical colouring, here are some natural alternatives. They might not be as bright as artificial colours, but they have their own style! They work best for icing.

RED Boil beetroot in enough water to cover it, then use the water as colouring (you can eat the beetroot!).

YELLOW Turmeric mixed with a little water.

GREEN Spirulina powder (from health-food shops) mixed with water. Or spinach: boil in water for a couple of minutes, then blend and sieve.

BLUE Boil red cabbage for 20 minutes in a little water. Reduce the liquid in a saucepan with the lid off. Cool, then add baking soda (not too much or it'll taste bad!)

PURPLE Blueberries: boil until reduced, then sieve.

Or you can buy natural food colouring online!

PINK Juice from frozen raspberries.

NATURAL DECORATIONS

Coloured sugar is a great alternative to edible glitter. Make your own with natural food colouring.

Grate chocolate with the fine side of a grater. Mix white and milk chocolate to make it look extra fancy!

Fruit makes colourful, healthy decorations.

Dried fruit and chopped nuts.

HOW TO MAKE NATURAL SPRINKLES

1) Mix unsweetened shredded coconut with natural food colouring.

2) Spread them out thinly and leave out to dry for 24 hours.

ICING TECHNIQUES

Use a reusable piping bag instead of disposable ones to save on waste. If you get one with a plastic 'coupler', you can change tips easily as you go.

Put the bag over a tall glass to make it easier to fill with buttercream.

buttercream in here!

Buttercream consistency is important.

Thick for flowers and thin ruffles.
Medium for big cupcake swirls.
Soft for writing and lines.

If your buttercream's **too soft**, add some icing sugar.

If it's **too thick**, add a teaspoon of milk.

WHAT ARE DIFFERENT PIPING TIPS FOR?

Large Round
Smooth swirls, blobs

Small Round
Writing, lines, dots

Star-Shaped
Textured swirls

Closed Star
Rosettes, swirls

Teardrop
Flower petals, ruffles

Grass Tip
Also good for fur!

Basketweave
Interlocking patterns

Leaf Tip
Leaves for flowers

ICING PATTERNS

Classic Ice Cream Style Swirl
Make it short or tall!

Rosette Swirl
Use a closed star tip and spiral outwards.

Multiple Swirls

Ruffles
Use a teardrop tip (round edge inward). Rotate the cake and swirl!

Shells
Use a star tip and make little loops.

Little Star Rosettes
Use a small star tip. Hold still, squeeze, then pull up.

Buttercream Mountain
Hold the piping bag vertically. Keep it still and squeeeeeze!

Perfect icing takes practice so don't get disheartened. And remember: even if it's a complete mess, it'll still be delicious!

WATERMELON CUPCAKES

For the cupcakes:
85 g (3 oz) butter (room temperature)
135 g (4¾ oz) caster sugar
3 free-range egg whites
120 ml (4 fl oz) sour cream
1 tsp vanilla extract
135 g (4¾ oz) plain flour
1½ tsp baking powder
pinch of salt
green food colouring

For the icing/decorations:
140 g (5 oz) butter (room temperature)
280 g (10 oz) icing sugar
watermelon flavouring (or syrup)
red food colouring
milk chocolate chips

FIRST MAKE THE CUPCAKES:

- Preheat the oven to 180°C / 160°C fan / gas 4 and line a 12-hole cupcake tray with cases.

- Beat the butter and sugar until fluffy.

- Beat in the egg whites.

- Mix in the sour cream and vanilla by hand.

- In a separate bowl, combine the flour, baking powder and salt.

- Gradually combine the dry and wet mixtures, then add a little green food colouring.

- Divide the mixture between the cases (two-thirds full) and bake for 15–20 minutes. Cool completely before icing.

NOW DECORATE!

1) Mix the butter and half the icing sugar until smooth. Then mix in the rest of the sugar and the watermelon flavouring/syrup.

2) Put the icing in a piping bag. Start in the centre of the cake and make a spiral outwards for the first layer.

Use a star-shaped icing tip.

3) Spiral back in to build up the second layer.

The shape we're aiming for is soft-serve ice cream!

4) Add chocolate chips as melon seeds!

Yum!

RAINBOW DREAMS

For the cupcakes:
240 g (8½ oz) plain flour
240 g (8½ oz) golden caster sugar
3 tsp baking powder
pinch of salt
80 g (2¾ oz) unsalted butter (room temperature)
240 ml (8½ fl oz) whole milk
2 free-range eggs
½ tsp vanilla extract
food colouring – at least 4 colours

For the cloud icing:
225 g (8 oz) full fat cream cheese*
125 g (4½ oz) icing sugar
1 tsp vanilla extract
550 ml (16 fl oz) whipping cream*

*Use straight from the fridge so they're cold.

FIRST MAKE THE CUPCAKES:

- Preheat the oven to 170°C / 150°C fan / gas 3 and line two 12-hole cupcake trays with cases.

- Mix together the flour, sugar, baking powder, salt & butter, then half the milk.

- In a separate bowl, mix the eggs, vanilla and the rest of the milk.

- Combine the two mixtures until smooth.

- Divide into separate bowls for each colour and add the food colouring!

- Layer into cake cases – be careful not to mix the colours together.

- Bake for 20–25 minutes. Leave to cool completely before decorating – or your clouds will melt!

Try out different colours! Go for layers or splodge different colours in patches.

I'm naked!

Extra magical rainbow inside!

1) Whisk the cream cheese and icing sugar together until smooth.

Use an electric mixer if you have one!

2) Add the vanilla and cream. Whip on slow until peaks form.

Anyone fancy skiing?

3) Use a piping bag with a large circle nozzle. Start in the centre of the cake and make loops to build up puffy clouds!

DOUBLE RAINBOW CAKES: Add rainbow belt gummy sweets!

WASABI & WHITE CHOCOLATE

For the cupcakes:
175 g (6¼ oz) self-raising flour
50 g (1¾ oz) plain flour
1 tsp baking powder
175 g (6¼ oz) unsalted butter (softened)
175 g (6¼ oz) caster sugar
3 large free-range eggs
2 tbsp milk
1 tbsp wasabi paste
100 g (3½ oz) white chocolate chips

For the icing:
125 g (4½ oz) butter (softened)
350 g (12¼ oz) icing sugar
3 tbsp milk
1 tsp vanilla extract
1–2 tsp wasabi paste (to taste)
green food colouring (optional)

FIRST MAKE THE CUPCAKES:

- Preheat the oven to 180°C / 160°C fan / gas 4 and line a 12-hole cupcake tray.

- In a large bowl, sift together the flours and baking powder. Set aside.

- Mix the butter and sugar in an electric mixer until light and creamy.

- Add the eggs one at a time, mixing well between each addition.

- Add the flour mixture and combine thoroughly.

- Stir in the milk and wasabi paste, then mix in the chocolate chips.

- Fill the cases two-thirds full and bake for 20–25 mins. Cool completely before icing.

Can you handle it?

He's not really that fearsome!

DANGER

NOW DECORATE!

1) Place the butter in the bowl of an electric mixer with the icing sugar. Mix on low to combine.

2) Still mixing slowly, add a little milk until it's the right consistency, then the vanilla extract, wasabi paste & food colouring.

Use food colouring if you want the icing to be green!

3) Swirl onto the cakes with a piping bag and enjoy!

Use a large round or open star tip.

STRAWBERRY SHORTCAKE

For the cupcakes:
200 g (7 oz) unsalted butter (softened)
200 g (7 oz) caster sugar
4 free-range eggs
200 g (7 oz) self-raising flour
4 tbsp strawberry jam
340 g (12 oz) strawberries, finely chopped
(keep a few whole for the topping)

For the icing/decorations:
350 ml (12½ fl oz) double cream
100 g (3½ oz) icing sugar

FIRST MAKE THE CUPCAKES:
- Preheat the oven to 200°C / 180°C fan / gas 6. Line two 12-hole cupcake trays with cases.

- Cream the butter and sugar together in a large bowl until light and fluffy.

- Beat in the eggs one at a time until well combined. If it looks like it's curdling, add a spoonful of flour. Fold in the rest of the flour until the mixture is soft and smooth.

- Whisk the jam in a small bowl until smooth. Fold in the chopped strawberries.

- Half-fill the cake cases with cake mix. Add half a teaspoon of jam mixture, then cover with cake mix. The cases should be ¾ full.

- Bake for 12–15 minutes. Cool completely before decorating.

In Japan this is Christmas cake!

I'm a mini version!

NOW DECORATE!

1) Whip the cream with the icing sugar. The sugar gives it more stability (and yummy sweetness!).

2) Use a piping bag with a medium closed star tip for the cream.

yay!

3) Pipe on the cream! First make a swirl in the middle.

BEST CUPCAKE

Then add rosettes around the edge.

4) Finally, the finishing touch: a delicious whole strawberry in the middle!

GREEN TEA MATCHA CUPCAKES

For the cupcakes:
175 g (6¼ oz) plain flour
¼ tsp salt
½ tsp bicarbonate of soda
1 tsp baking powder
170 g (6 oz) caster sugar
2 tbsp matcha green tea powder
170 ml (6 fl oz) buttermilk
115 ml (4 fl oz) vegetable oil
1 large free-range egg
½ tsp vanilla extract

For the icing/decorations:
225 ml (8 fl oz) whipping or double cream
½ tsp vanilla extract
55 g (2 oz) caster sugar
1 tsp matcha green tea powder

FIRST MAKE THE CUPCAKES:
- Preheat the oven to 175°C / 155°C fan / gas 3. Line a 12-hole cupcake tray with cases.

- In a small bowl, combine the flour, salt, bicarbonate of soda, baking powder, sugar and matcha green tea powder with a whisk and set aside.

- In a medium bowl, whisk the buttermilk, oil, egg and vanilla extract together. Gradually add the flour mixture while slowly whisking until combined — take care not to overmix or they will be tough.

- Divide the mixture between the cases and bake for 15–17 minutes.

- Cool completely before icing.

Tea & cake: perfect partners!

NOW DECORATE!

1) Matcha is made of powdered green tea leaves. It has lots of health benefits and a slightly bitter taste that goes well with sweetness (like cake and buttercream!).

Matcha powder is whisked to make tea.

2) To make the icing, beat the cream, vanilla extract & sugar together until peaks form.

SWIRL

3) Pipe the icing onto the cupcakes using a large round tip.

Start at the edge & spiral up!

...dizzy...

4) Dust with matcha powder using a sieve.

It's snowing!!

CHERRY BLOSSOM CUPCAKES

For the cupcakes:
140 g (5 oz) plain flour
40 g (1½ oz) ground almonds
1 tsp baking powder
¼ tsp bicarbonate of soda
½ tsp salt
160 ml (5¾ fl oz) vegetable oil
240 ml (8½ fl oz) almond (or cow's) milk
½ tbsp cider vinegar
½ tsp vanilla extract
150 g (5¼ oz) caster sugar

For the icing/decorations:
180 g (6¼ oz) butter (room temperature)
250 g (8¾ oz) icing sugar
a few drops of sakura (cherry blossom)
extract or cherry juice

FIRST MAKE THE CUPCAKES:

- Preheat the oven to 180°C / 160°C fan / gas 4. Line a 12-hole cupcake tray with cases.

- Mix together the flour, almonds, baking powder, bicarbonate of soda and salt in a large bowl and set aside.

- Separately, whisk together the oil, milk, vinegar and vanilla extract.

- Add the sugar and mix until combined.

- Combine the wet and dry ingredients and mix until combined (it'll be slightly lumpy and quite thin).

- Divide the mixture between the cases (about two-thirds full). Bake for 20–22 minutes. Cool completely before icing.

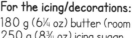

If you can't get cherry blossom extract, use cherry juice, or juice from frozen cherries.

We're close relatives!

NOW DECORATE!

1) Beat the butter and icing sugar until pale and fluffy to make a buttercream. Saving half of it for the decorations, spread the other half of the buttercream onto the cupcakes with a palette knife, or the flat back edge of any knife.

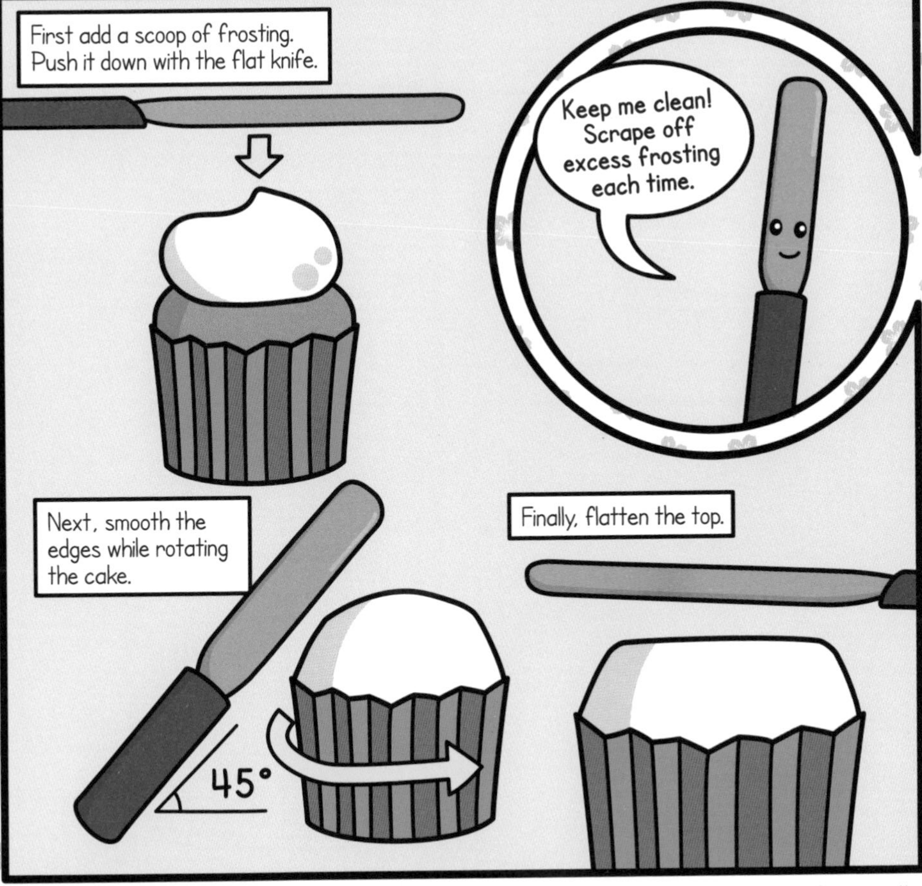
First add a scoop of frosting. Push it down with the flat knife.
Keep me clean! Scrape off excess frosting each time.
Next, smooth the edges while rotating the cake.
45°
Finally, flatten the top.

2) Divide the remaining buttercream into two small bowls. Add a few drops of sakura essence or cherry juice to make one pale pink and one darker pink.

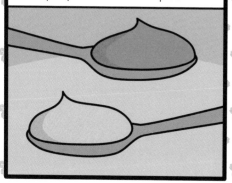

3) Get your piping bag and a teardrop-shaped tip. Put the dark pink buttercream along one side of the bag, then fill the rest with the lighter buttercream.

I'm so sad ...

darker pink
light pink

4) Time to make the blossoms! Hold the cake in one hand and the icing bag in the other.

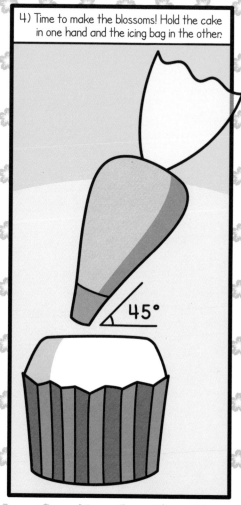

45°

5) Keep the rounded edge of the teardrop tip at the centre of the flower. Make a little swirl for each petal. Rotate the cake as you go, to make the whole blossom.

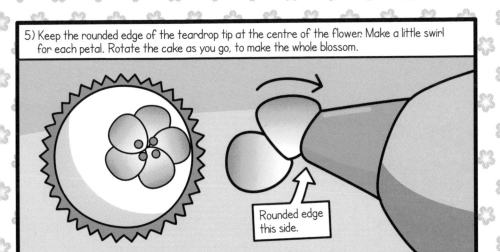

Rounded edge this side.

6) Use a small round tip to add a couple of tiny dots of darker pink buttercream at the centre of each blossom.

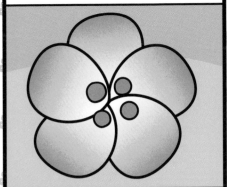

7) Add a couple of blossoms on each cake. Now you're ready for hanami!

Hanami is cherry-blossom viewing in Japan! Time for picnics under the fluffy pink cherry trees.

PINATA CUPCAKES

For the cupcakes:

210 g (7½ oz) plain flour
1½ tsp baking powder
¼ tsp salt
55 g (2 oz) unsalted butter (room temp.)
60 ml (2¼ oz) vegetable oil
170 g (6 oz) caster sugar
2 large free-range eggs (room temp.)
1½ tsp vanilla extract
150 ml (5¼ fl oz) buttermilk

For the icing/filling:

225 g (8 oz) icing sugar
60 g (2¼ oz) butter
a few drops of vanilla extract
2 different food colourings
50 g (1¾ oz) mini chocolate beans

FIRST MAKE THE CUPCAKES:

- Preheat the oven to 175°C / 155°C fan / gas 3. Line a 12-hole cupcake tray.

- Mix the flour, baking powder and salt together in a bowl and set aside.

- In a separate bowl, beat together the butter, oil and sugar until well combined. Add the eggs one at a time, beating well after each one. Stir in the vanilla extract.

- Alternate adding the flour mixture and buttermilk to the butter mixture. Start with the flour and mix until just combined each time. It should be smooth, but try not to over-mix.

- Divide between the cupcake cases. Fill each one two-thirds full.

- Bake for 15–17 minutes. Cool before icing.

Secret treasure middle!

AND extra magical frosting!

NOW DECORATE!

1) Cut a circle out of each cupcake to make a secret compartment about 2.5 cm deep.

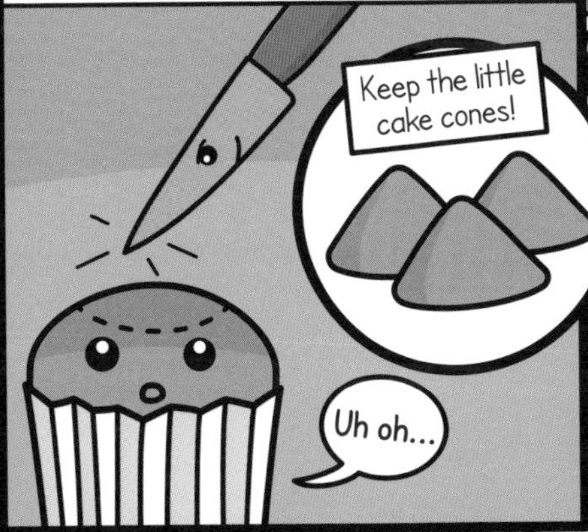
Keep the little cake cones!
Uh oh...

2) Hide the secret chocolate beans in the holes. Slice off the top of each cake cone and use as lids to seal them up!

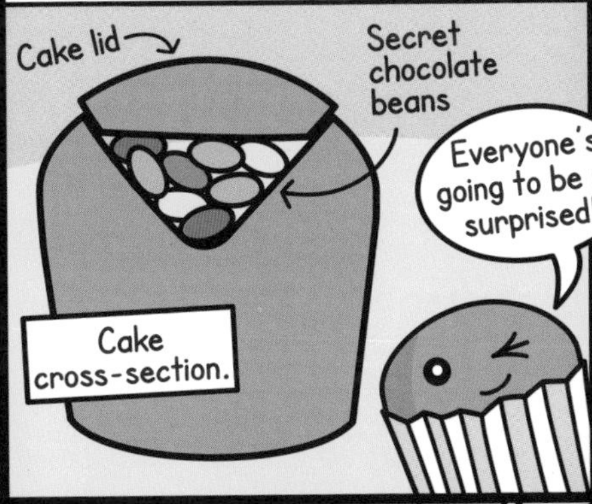
Cake lid
Secret chocolate beans
Everyone's going to be so surprised!
Cake cross-section.

3) Mix the butter with the icing sugar and vanilla extract to make a buttercream. Divide it in two and add a different food colouring to each one.

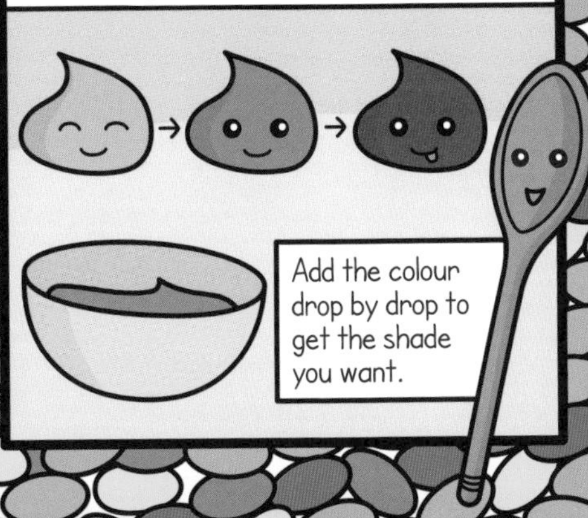
Add the colour drop by drop to get the shade you want.

4) Put one colour buttercream in each side of the piping bag. Swirl it onto the cakes to hide the secret compartment!

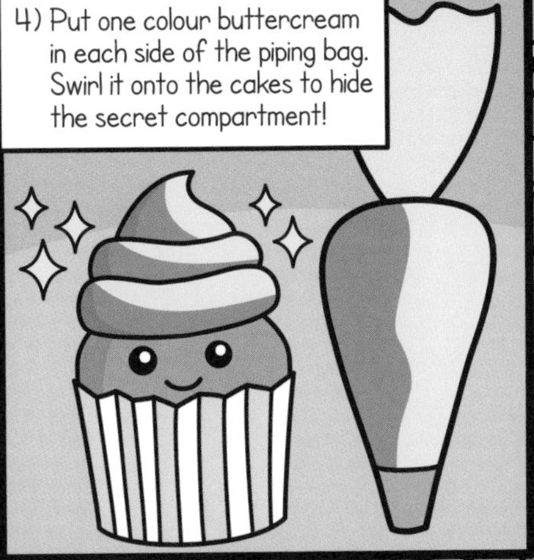

GINGERBREAD MICROWAVE MUG CAKE

For the mug cake:
2 tbsp butter
2 tbsp runny honey
1 medium free-range egg
½ tsp vanilla extract
3 tbsp light brown sugar
4 tbsp self-raising flour
½ tsp ground ginger
pinch of salt

For the icing:
2 tbsp butter (softened)
3 tbsp icing sugar
½ tsp runny honey

FIRST MAKE THE CUPCAKES:

- Put the butter in a mug and melt in the microwave for 10 – 20 seconds.
- Add the honey, egg and vanilla and beat with a fork until combined.
- Add the sugar, flour, ground ginger and salt. Beat until smooth and fully combined.
- Cook in the microwave for 1 minute 15 seconds to 1 minute 30 seconds (depending on your microwave's power).
- Allow to cool before icing.

Cake in a mug!

1) Mug cakes are quick to make, for all those times when you just need cake – fast!

2) If you can wait till it's cooled down, make it extra special with a swirl of yummy honey buttercream icing.

3) We're going to mix the icing in a mug too! Add the butter, icing sugar and honey. Mash the butter with a fork, then beat the icing until fluffy.

4) Spoon the icing into a piping bag with an open star tip, and swirl it onto the cake!

FUNFETTI CUPCAKES

For the cupcakes:

½ tsp salt
3 tsp baking powder
280 g (10 oz) plain flour
225 g (8 oz) unsalted butter (melted)
340 g (12 oz) caster sugar
4 large free-range eggs
1 tbsp vanilla extract
280 ml (10 fl oz) buttermilk
150 g (5¼ oz) multi-coloured sprinkles

For the icing:

225 g (8 oz) unsalted butter (softened)
560 g (19¾ oz) icing sugar
½ tsp salt
1 tsp vanilla extract
3 tbsp whipping or double cream

FIRST MAKE THE CUPCAKES:

- Preheat the oven to 175°C / 155°C fan / gas 3. Prepare a 12-hole cupcake tray.
- Whisk the salt, baking powder and flour in a medium-sized bowl. Set aside.
- In a separate bowl, beat the butter and sugar until smooth. Beat in the eggs one by one, then add the vanilla extract.
- Add the dry ingredients alternately with the buttermilk, starting and ending with the flour. Mix gently as you add each one.
- Stir in the sprinkles.
- Divide the mixture between the cases (two-thirds full). Bake for 14–17 minutes.
- Cool completely before icing.

A party in a cupcake!

NOW DECORATE!

1) Funfetti cupcakes have sprinkles inside and out!

2) For the icing, beat the butter until smooth. Add the icing sugar bit by bit and beat on medium speed until crumbly. Mix in the salt & vanilla. Add 1 tablespoon of cream at a time. Keep mixing until it's smooth.

3) Swirl on the icing with a piping bag and a large circle tip.

4) It wouldn't be complete without sprinkles … and MORE sprinkles!!!

LADYBIRD CUPCAKES

For the cupcakes:

100 g (3½ oz) plain flour
20 g (¾ oz) cocoa powder
140 g (5 oz) caster sugar
1½ tsp baking powder
40 g (1½ oz) unsalted butter (room temp.)
pinch of salt
120 ml (2¼ fl oz) whole milk
1 large free-range egg
¼ tsp vanilla extract

For the icing/decorations:

600 g (21 oz) icing sugar, sifted
300 g (10½ oz) butter (softened)
red and black food colouring
candy eyes

FIRST MAKE THE CUPCAKES:

- Preheat the oven to 180°C / 160°C fan / gas 4. Line a 12-hole cupcake tray.

- Mix the flour, cocoa powder, sugar, baking powder, butter and a pinch of salt together until combined.

- Whisk the milk, egg and vanilla extract together in a jug. Then add half to the flour mixture.

- Beat to combine and turn the mixer up to high speed. Then add the remaining liquid. Continue mixing for a few more minutes until smooth.

- Divide the mixture between the cases (two-thirds full).

- Bake for 20–25 minutes. Allow to cool completely before icing.

NOW DECORATE!

1) Mix the icing sugar and butter together and beat until smooth. Divide into two bowls: two thirds in one and one third in the other. Add food colouring drop by drop to get the right shade.

I'm going to be the ladybird's spots!

two thirds red

one third black

Add RED food colouring to the larger bowl.

Add BLACK food colouring to the smaller bowl.

2) Cover the cupcakes with the red buttercream.

Sides first, then the top.

Put a scoop of red icing on the cake.

Spread it over the whole surface.

Use the back of the knife to smooth it down in small sweeps. Scrape excess icing off the knife after each sweep.

3) Put the black icing in a piping bag. Use a round tip to draw the head, wings, antennae and spots.

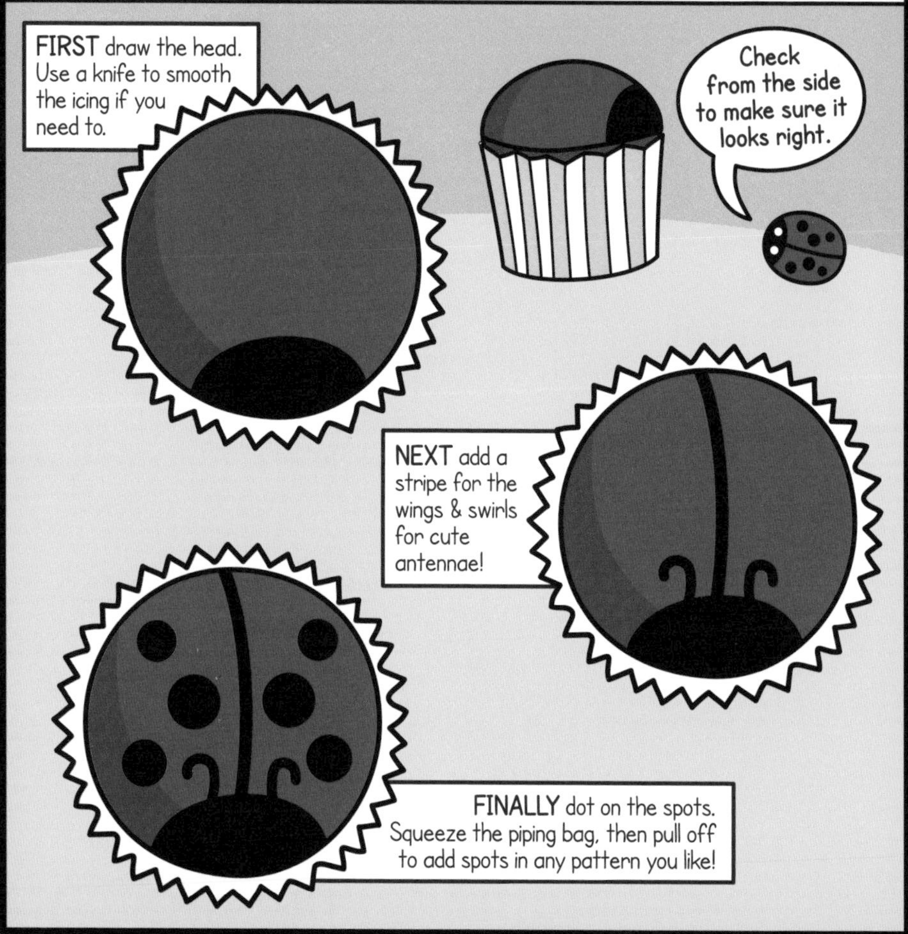
FIRST draw the head. Use a knife to smooth the icing if you need to.
Check from the side to make sure it looks right.
NEXT add a stripe for the wings & swirls for cute antennae!
FINALLY dot on the spots. Squeeze the piping bag, then pull off to add spots in any pattern you like!

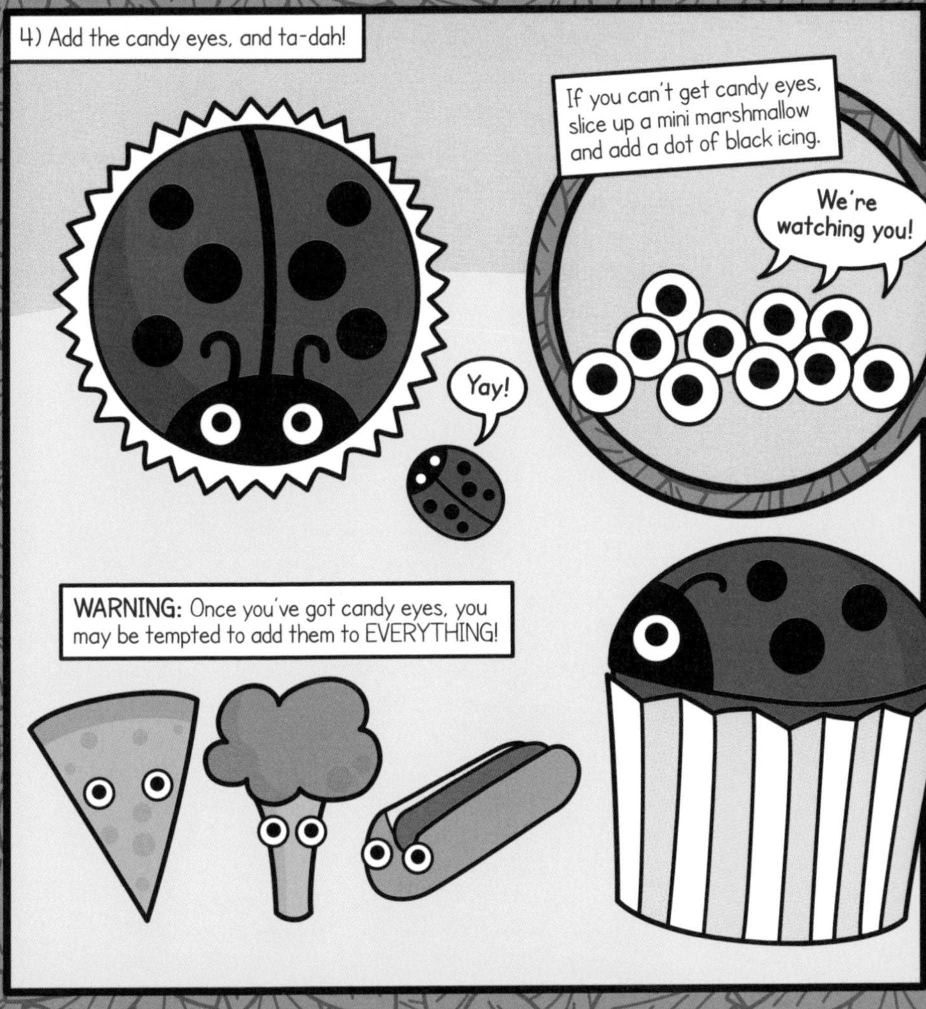
4) Add the candy eyes, and ta-dah!
If you can't get candy eyes, slice up a mini marshmallow and add a dot of black icing.
We're watching you!
Yay!
WARNING: Once you've got candy eyes, you may be tempted to add them to EVERYTHING!

MAPLE PANCAKE CUPCAKES

For the cupcakes:
225 g (8 oz) butter (softened)
340 g (12 oz) sugar
3 large free-range eggs
2 large free-range egg whites
490 g (17¼ oz) plain flour
½ tsp nutmeg
1 tsp bicarbonate of soda
½ tsp baking powder
1 tsp salt
75 ml (2½ fl oz) milk
1 tbsp vanilla extract
100 g (3½ oz) sour cream
240 g (8½ oz) blueberries
(fresh or frozen)

For the icing/decorations:
115 g (4 oz) butter (softened)
225 g (8 oz) cream cheese
2 tsp maple extract or flavouring
560 g (19¾ oz) icing sugar
a little milk
cinnamon sugar
blueberries

FIRST MAKE THE CUPCAKES:

- Preheat the oven to 175°C / 155°C fan / gas 3. Line two 12-hole cupcake trays with cases.

- Beat the butter and sugar until light and fluffy. Add the eggs and egg whites one at a time until combined.

- In one bowl, sift the flour, nutmeg, bicarbonate of soda, baking powder & salt. In another bowl combine the milk, vanilla & sour cream.

- Add the dry ingredients to the butter mixture a third at a time, alternating with the milk, vanilla extract and sour cream. Combine each one fully before adding the next. Don't over-mix.

- Fold in the blueberries then divide the mix between the cases (¾ full). Bake for 16–18 minutes. Cool completely before icing.

NOW DECORATE!

1) For the buttercream, beat the butter and cream cheese until light and fluffy. Add the maple syrup and icing sugar & beat again.

You can't have pancakes without syrup!

Add a little milk if it's too thick.

2) Pipe the buttercream onto the cupcakes in a big swirl.

Definitely not flat as a pancake ...

3) Sprinkle with cinnamon sugar and yummy blueberries.

wheee!!!

PINK LEMONADE CUPCAKES

For the cupcakes:

125 g (4½ oz) butter (softened)
220 g (7¾ oz) caster sugar
1 tbsp lemon zest (finely grated)
2 large free-range eggs
225 g (8 oz) self-raising flour
120 ml (4¼ fl oz) sour cream
2 tbsp lemon juice
160 g (5½ oz) lemon curd

For the icing/decorations:

250 g (8¾ oz) butter (softened)
500 g (17½ oz) icing sugar
2 tbsp raspberry cordial plus extra for drizzling!
1 lemon (sliced)

FIRST MAKE THE CUPCAKES:

- Preheat oven to 180°C / 160°C fan / gas 4. Line a 12-hole cupcake tray with cases.

- Beat the butter, sugar and lemon zest in a bowl until pale and creamy.

- Add the eggs one at a time, beating well after each addition.

- Stir in the flour.

- Add the sour cream and lemon juice. Stir to combine.

- Add the lemon curd and gently fold to marble.

- Divide the mixture evenly among the paper cases. Bake for 20–25 minutes. Cool completely before icing.

Sweet and sour!

NOW DECORATE!

1) To make the pink buttercream, beat the butter in a bowl until pale. Gradually beat in the icing sugar in batches. Add the raspberry cordial and mix until combined.

2) Spoon the buttercream into a piping bag. Use a large star-shaped tip and pipe spirals onto the cupcakes.

3) Drizzle with raspberry cordial.

4) Garnish with a lemon slice for the finishing touch!

STARRY NIGHT CUPCAKES WITH SPACE DUST

For the cupcakes:
150 g (5¼ oz) unsalted butter (softened)
150 g (5¼ oz) golden caster sugar
3 large free-range eggs
½ tsp baking powder
150 g (5¼ oz) self-raising flour
½ tsp vanilla extract

For the icing/decorations:
80 g (3 oz) unsalted butter (softened)
250 g (8¾ oz) icing sugar
1 tsp vanilla extract
purple and blue food colouring
magical sparkly decorations: edible glitter, sprinkles, stars or coloured sugar

A whole galaxy of cupcakes!

FIRST MAKE THE CUPCAKES:
- Preheat the oven to 180°C / 160°C fan / gas 4. Line a 12-hole cupcake tray with cases.
- Beat together the butter and sugar until light and fluffy.
- One by one, add the eggs, baking powder, flour and vanilla extract, and beat until combined.
- Spoon the mixture into the cupcake cases, filling them two-thirds full.
- Bake for 20–25 minutes.
- Allow to cool completely before icing.

NOW DECORATE!

1) Beat together the butter, icing sugar and vanilla extract to make a buttercream.

2) Divide into two bowls. Add purple colouring to one and blue colouring to the other, then mix it in well.

3) Fill half the piping bag with the blue buttercream and the other half with the purple buttercream.

4) Pipe icing spirals onto the cupcakes.

5) Decorate the cupcakes with sparkly decorations for stars and galaxies. Just sprinkle them on – space is random so you don't have to be too precise! Here are some ideas for decorations:

crackle

Sprinkles
You can get all sorts of mixtures!

Popping candy
Sprinkle on at the last minute so it doesn't lose its crackle!

Chocolate stars

Make your own super-sweet galaxy!

Round chocolates or candy
Add some planets! You could even pipe on a thin stripe for the rings.

Edible glitter or coloured sugar
Make sure it says edible on the label, not "for decorative purposes only"!

MAKE YOUR OWN
COLOURED SUGAR

1) Put the sugar in a box or jar with a lid. Add a couple of drops of food colouring.

I wish I was more colourful ...

Food colouring gel mixed with a couple of drops of water gives a brighter colour.

2) Shake for about 1 minute to distribute the colour (it's a workout!).

urgggg...

3) Spread it out on a plate and leave out overnight to dry.

And relax ...

... and you're done! It's sparkly like glitter – perfect for starry night cupcakes!

PANDA CUPCAKES

For the cupcakes:
105 g (3¾ oz) self-raising flour
95 g (3¼ oz) plain flour
125 g (4½ oz) unsalted butter (softened)
200 g (7 oz) caster sugar
2 large free-range eggs (room temperature)
115 ml (4 fl oz) milk
1 tsp vanilla extract

For the icing/decorations:
a dusting of icing sugar
white fondant
chocolate fondant
chocolate buttons

FIRST MAKE THE CUPCAKES:
- Preheat oven to 180°C / 160°C fan / gas 4. Line a 12-hole cupcake tray with cases.
- Combine the flours in a small bowl and set aside.
- Cream the butter in a large bowl until smooth.
- Gradually add the caster sugar and beat until fluffy.
- Add the eggs one at a time, beating well after each.
- Add the flour in 3 parts, alternating with the milk and vanilla. Each time, beat until the ingredients are incorporated.
- Divide the mixture between the cases, filling them about ¾ full.
- Bake for 20–25 minutes. Cool completely before decorating.

NOW DECORATE!

1) Start with the white fondant. Dust your work surface with icing sugar so it doesn't stick, and roll it out.

Knead the fondant first, so it's easier to roll.

Massage?

urg ...

2) Cut out large circles for the faces using a round cutter or knife.

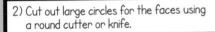

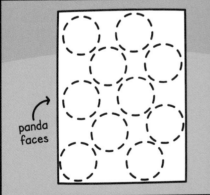

panda faces

3) Use the off-cuts to make small dots for the eyes.

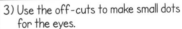

Sparkles make eyes look cuter!

4) Next roll out the chocolate fondant and cut out shapes for the panda eyes.

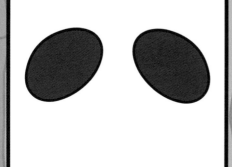

5) Shape the off-cuts into triangles for the noses and thin strings for the mouths.

panda noses

panda mouths

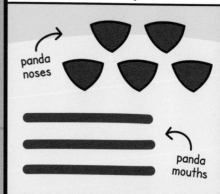

6) Carefully cut the tops off the cupcakes, so they're flat on top. (You can eat the off-cuts!)

7) Here's the best bit – put together the faces and see the pandas come to life!

Use jam as glue if you need to (or sugar glue)!

Add chocolate buttons for the ears.

Take a small ball of fondant and a teaspoon of water.

Microwave for 15–20 seconds.

If it's too thick, add a tiny drop of water and microwave for a few more seconds.

Stuck!

CARAMEL HONEYCOMB CUPCAKES

For the cupcakes:
150 g (5¼ oz) unsalted butter (room temperature)
150 g (5¼ oz) light muscovado sugar
3 large free-range eggs, beaten
150 g (5¼ oz) self-raising flour
½ tsp baking powder
1 tsp vanilla extract

For the icing/decorations:
60 g (2 oz) unsalted butter
250 g (8¾ oz) golden icing sugar
3 tbsp dulce de leche caramel sauce
pinch of salt (optional)
honeycomb chocolate bars

buzzzz!!

FIRST MAKE THE CUPCAKES:
- Preheat the oven to 180°C / 160°C fan / gas 4. Line a 12-hole cupcake tray with cases.
- Beat the butter and sugar together in a mixing bowl until light and fluffy.
- Gradually beat in the eggs one at a time until combined. Add a little flour if the mixture curdles.
- Add the flour, baking powder and vanilla extract and combine.
- Divide the mixture between the cases (two-thirds full). Bake for 20–25 minutes. Cool completely before icing.

NOW DECORATE!

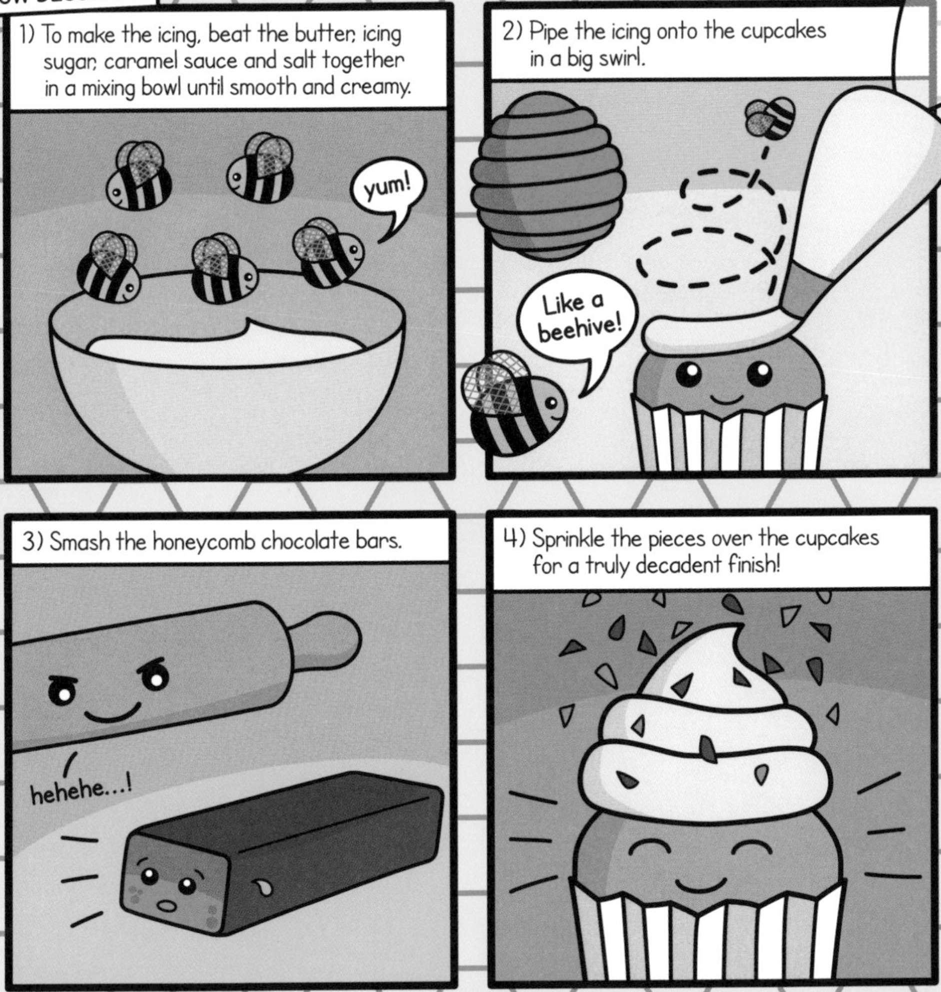
1) To make the icing, beat the butter, icing sugar, caramel sauce and salt together in a mixing bowl until smooth and creamy.
yum!
2) Pipe the icing onto the cupcakes in a big swirl.
Like a beehive!
3) Smash the honeycomb chocolate bars.
hehehe...!
4) Sprinkle the pieces over the cupcakes for a truly decadent finish!

BUNNY CARROT CAKES

For the cupcakes:

275 g (9¾ oz) caster sugar
200 ml (7 fl oz) sunflower oil
4 medium free-range eggs
300 g (10½ oz) grated carrot
150 g (5¼ oz) nuts or dried fruit (optional)
225 g (8 oz) spelt or wholemeal flour
2 tsp baking powder
1 tsp ground cinnamon
1 tsp mixed spice
1 tbsp cocoa powder

For the icing/decorations:

100 g (3½ oz) unsalted butter (softened)
250 g (8¾ oz) full-fat cream cheese
500 g (17½ oz) icing sugar (approx.)
milk chocolate
chocolate drops
mini marshmallows

FIRST MAKE THE CUPCAKES:

- Preheat oven to 180°C / 160°C fan / gas 4. Line a 12-hole cupcake tray with cases.

- Beat the sugar, oil and eggs together until smooth.

- Stir in the grated carrot and the chopped nuts or dried fruit (optional).

- In a separate bowl, combine the flour, baking powder, cinnamon, mixed spice and cocoa powder so they're evenly mixed. Then add to the carrot mixture.

- Divide the mixture between the cases (two-thirds full). Bake for 22–25 minutes. Cool completely before icing.

With marshmallow tails!

NOW DECORATE!

1) First make the chocolate bunny ears! Cover a baking tray with greaseproof paper.

2) Melt the chocolate in the microwave, 10 seconds at a time, stirring until it's fully melted.

Be careful! Chocolate burns easily!

For white ears, use white chocolate instead.

3) With a palette knife or small spoon, make ear shapes with chocolate on the paper.

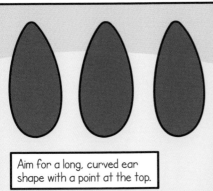

Aim for a long, curved ear shape with a point at the top.

4) Leave the tray in the fridge to set.

Brrr!!!

5) Once the chocolate's set, peel the ears off the paper and they're ready to use.

It's not every day you have a tray of ears...!

You can make chocolate drops like this too, if you want to add eyes! Just spot little dobs of chocolate on the paper.

6) Cream-cheese frosting goes really well with carrot cake! Beat the butter and cream cheese together in a bowl until combined. Add the icing sugar and whisk briefly until smooth.

BEST FRIENDS

7) Pipe the frosting onto the cupcakes in a swirl.

Because the frosting contains cream cheese, you'll need to keep it in the fridge.

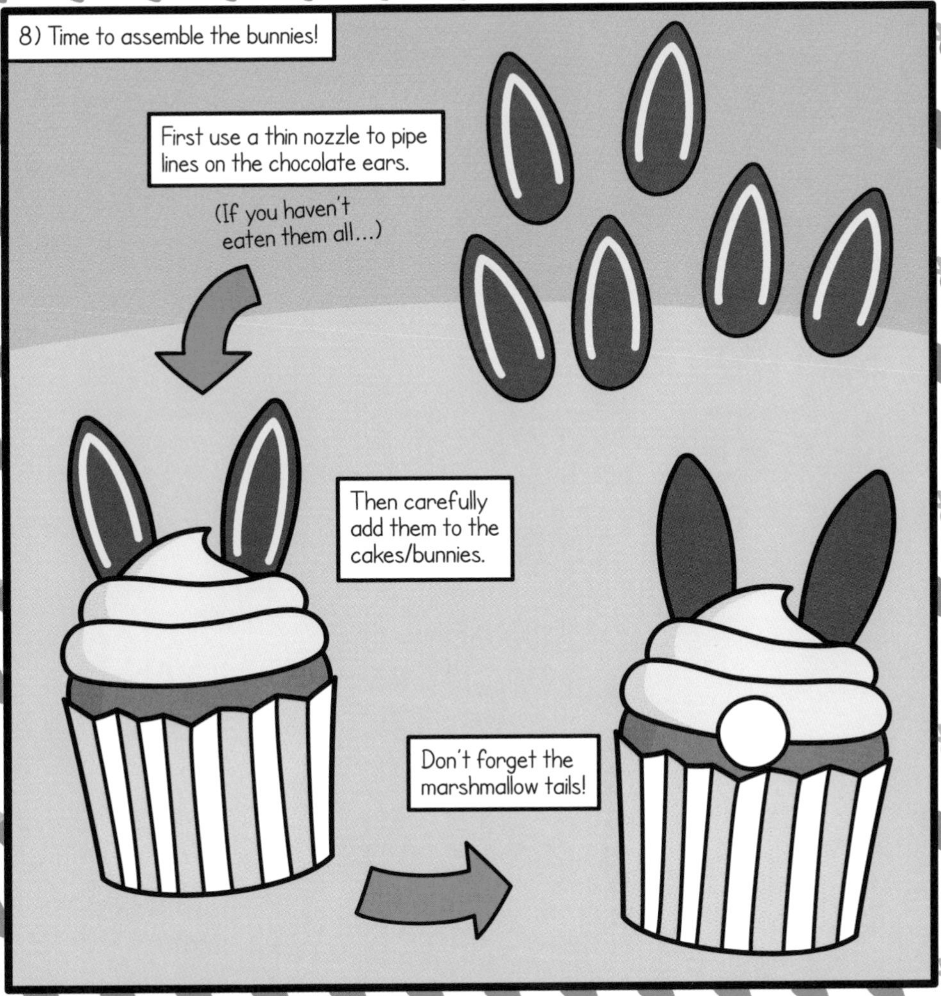
8) Time to assemble the bunnies!
First use a thin nozzle to pipe lines on the chocolate ears.
(If you haven't eaten them all...)
Then carefully add them to the cakes/bunnies.
Don't forget the marshmallow tails!

POLAR BEAR CUPCAKES

For the cupcakes:
100 g (3½ oz) plain flour
20 g (¾ oz) cocoa powder
140 g (5 oz) caster sugar
1½ tsp baking powder
40 g (1½ oz) unsalted butter (room temp.)
pinch of salt
120 ml (4 fl oz) whole milk
1 large free-range egg
¼ tsp vanilla extract

For the icing/decorations:
600 g (21 oz) icing sugar (sifted)
300 g (10½ oz) butter (softened)
100 g (3½ oz) large white chocolate buttons
100 g (3½ oz) small milk chocolate chips
large and small marshmallows

FIRST MAKE THE CUPCAKES:
- Preheat oven to 180°C / 160°C fan / gas 4. Prepare a 12-hole cupcake tray.
- Beat the flour, cocoa powder, sugar, baking powder, butter and a pinch of salt together on a slow speed until combined.
- Whisk the milk, egg and vanilla extract together in a jug.
- Slowly pour about half the milk and egg mixture into the flour mixture. Beat to combine and turn the mixer up to high speed. Then add the remaining liquid and mix for a few more minutes until smooth.
- Divide the mixture between the cases (two-thirds full). Bake for 20–25 minutes. Cool completely before icing.

NOW DECORATE!

1) Beat the icing sugar and butter together until smooth. Spread the buttercream onto the cupcakes. First smooth it roughly with a knife to cover the cake, then fluff it up like fur!

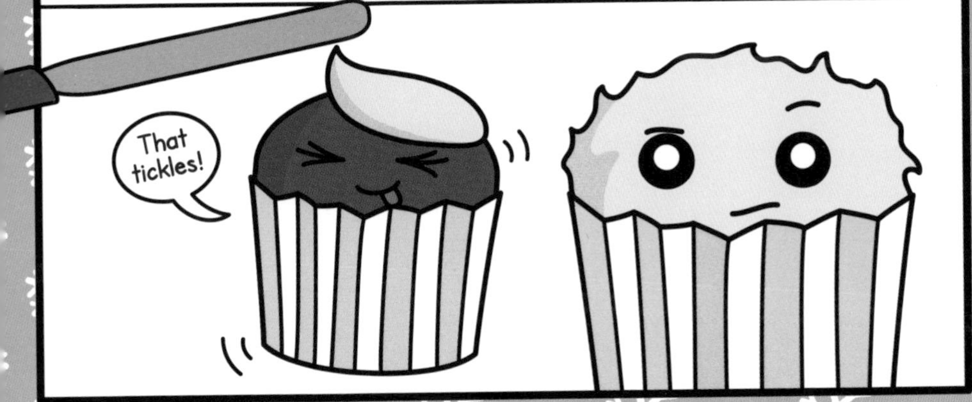
That tickles!

2) Now it's time to make the faces! Use buttercream as glue.

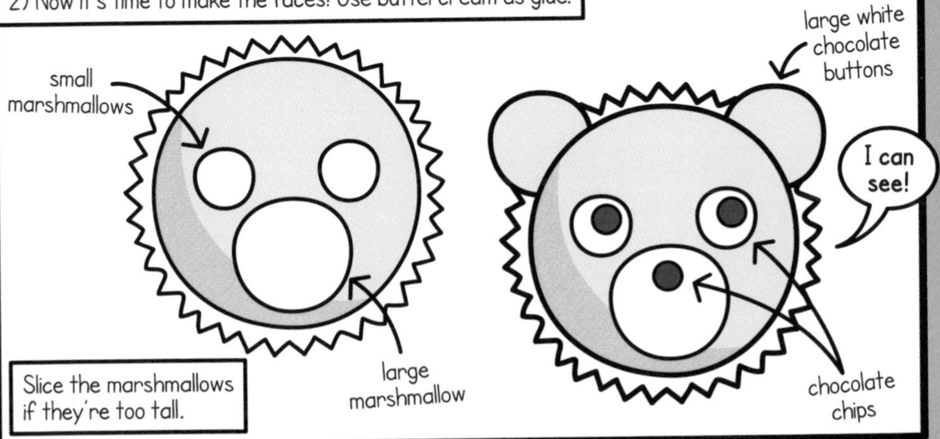
small marshmallows
large marshmallow
large white chocolate buttons
I can see!
chocolate chips

Slice the marshmallows if they're too tall.

HALLOWEEN RED VELVET CAKES

For the cupcakes:

350 g (12¼ oz) plain flour
1 tsp baking powder
½ tsp salt
38 ml (1½ oz) red food colouring
3½ tbsp unsweetened cocoa powder
115 g (4 oz) unsalted butter (softened)
340 g (12 oz) sugar
2 large free-range eggs (room temp.)
1 tsp vanilla extract
225 ml (8 oz) buttermilk (room temp.)
1 tsp white vinegar
1 tsp baking soda

For the icing ('blood' sauce):

200 g (7 oz) white chocolate
150 g (5¼ oz) unsalted butter
250 g (8¾ oz) mascarpone
210 g (7½ oz) icing sugar (sifted)
200 g (7 oz) raspberries or strawberries
(fresh or frozen)
1 tbsp icing sugar
red food colouring

FIRST MAKE THE CUPCAKES:

- Preheat the oven to 180°C / 160°C fan / gas 4. Line two 12-hole cupcake trays with cases.

- Sift the flour, baking powder and salt together.

- In another bowl, mix the red food colouring and cocoa powder into a thin paste.

- In a large bowl, beat butter and sugar together until light and fluffy.

- Beat in the eggs, one at a time.

- Mix in the vanilla and food colouring paste.

- Add one third of the flour mixture to the butter mixture and mix well.

- Beat in half of the buttermilk, then the rest of the flour mixture, followed by the remaining buttermilk, until well combined.

- In a small bowl, mix the vinegar and baking soda (it will fizz!), then add to the cake mix and stir well to combine.

- Divide the mixture between the cases (two-thirds full). Bake for 18–20 minutes. Cool completely before icing.

NOW DECORATE!

1) If it's not Halloween season, you can make a regular, non-scary version — just leave off the 'blood sauce' (unless you're a vampire ... or you really like strawberries!).

2) Melt the white chocolate in a heatproof bowl over simmering water. Remove from the heat so it cools slightly, but stays liquid.

3) In a cauldron*, mix the butter on medium speed until light and creamy. Add the mascarpone and mix until fluffy. Add the melted white chocolate and mix well.

*mixing bowl

4) Gradually add the icing sugar until you have the right consistency. Pipe onto the cupcakes.

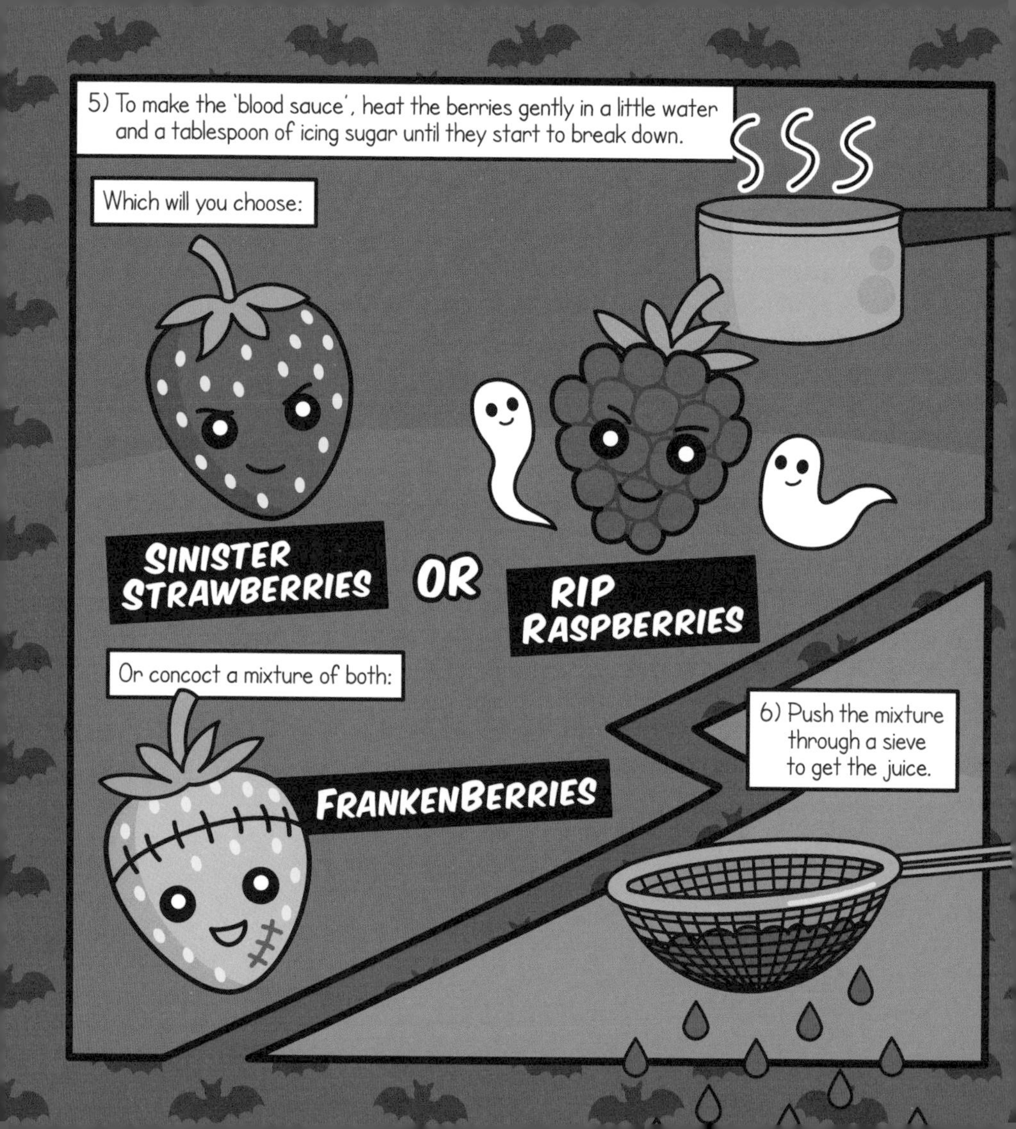
5) To make the 'blood sauce', heat the berries gently in a little water and a tablespoon of icing sugar until they start to break down.
Which will you choose:
SINISTER STRAWBERRIES
OR
RIP RASPBERRIES
Or concoct a mixture of both:
FRANKENBERRIES
6) Push the mixture through a sieve to get the juice.

7) Add a few drops of red food colouring and mix well. Add a little water if necessary for a syrup-y (blood) consistency. Drizzle over the cupcakes (preferably at midnight!) while chanting your best spells and incantations!

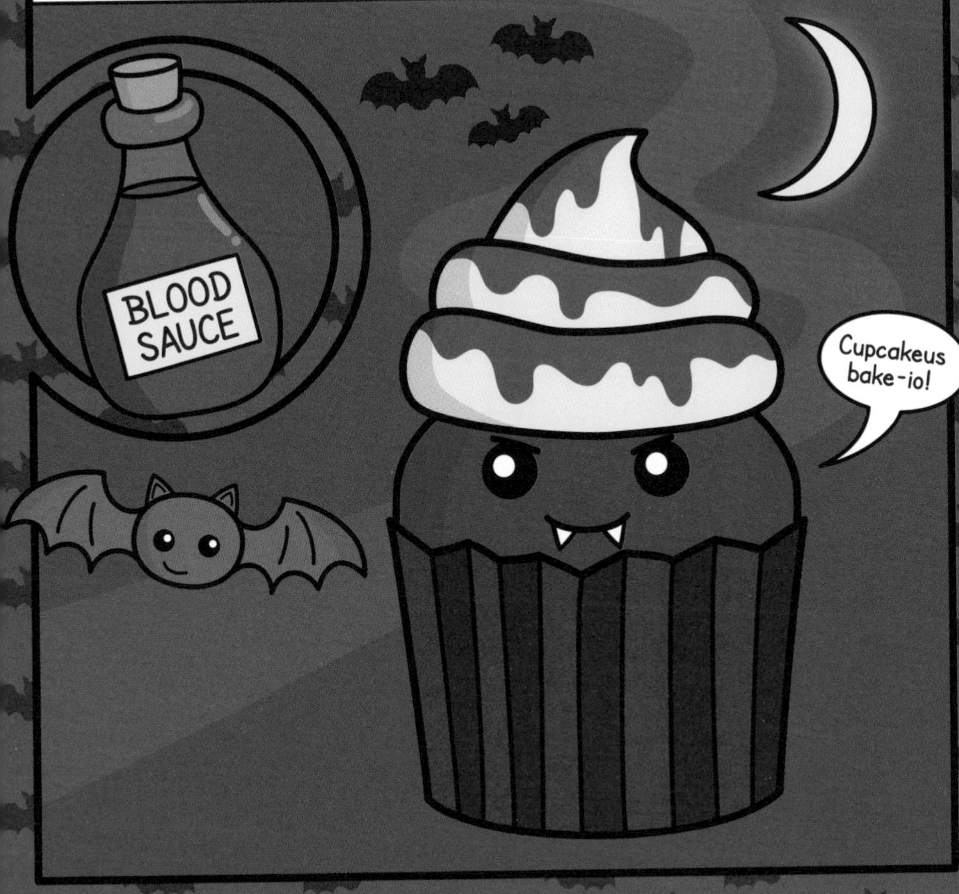
BLOOD SAUCE
Cupcakeus bake-io!

CUPCAKE TROUBLE-SHOOTING

Sinking middle
Make sure you're adding the ingredients in the right order, and try not to over-mix.

Cracked top
The oven's too hot. Use a lower shelf, or lower the temperature slightly.

Overflowing cupcakes
Only fill your cases two-thirds full. It could be that the oven's too hot. Or too much baking powder has been used.

Cupcakes don't rise
It could be your flour or baking powder. Is it still in date? Perhaps try a different brand.

Lumpy mixture
The butter's too cold. Let it warm up to room temperature before you start. Remember to sift the flour through a sieve so it all mixes in.

Dense texture
The butter might have been too soft. It should be softened, but not too squidgy!

Sinking chocolate chips, raisins, etc.

This might be caused by over-mixing (which makes the mixture thinner).
Or try rolling them in flour before adding them.

Peeling cases

Most likely caused by too much moisture when the cakes are stored.
Make sure the cakes are cooled completely before you put them away.
Or try different cases!

It's my 'just got back from holiday' look

REMEMBER

Don't open the oven door until the cakes are done! Resist the temptation to check on them halfway through; letting cool air in will make your cakes sink in the middle.

Too pale or too brown

Every oven is different, so you might need to adjust the temperature or cooking time slightly. Check they're cooked with a skewer – it should come out clean.

Drooping icing

Consistency is very important when you're piping icing.
If it's drooping, it needs to be thicker. Add more icing sugar to make your icing thicker, or a spoonful of milk to make it thinner.

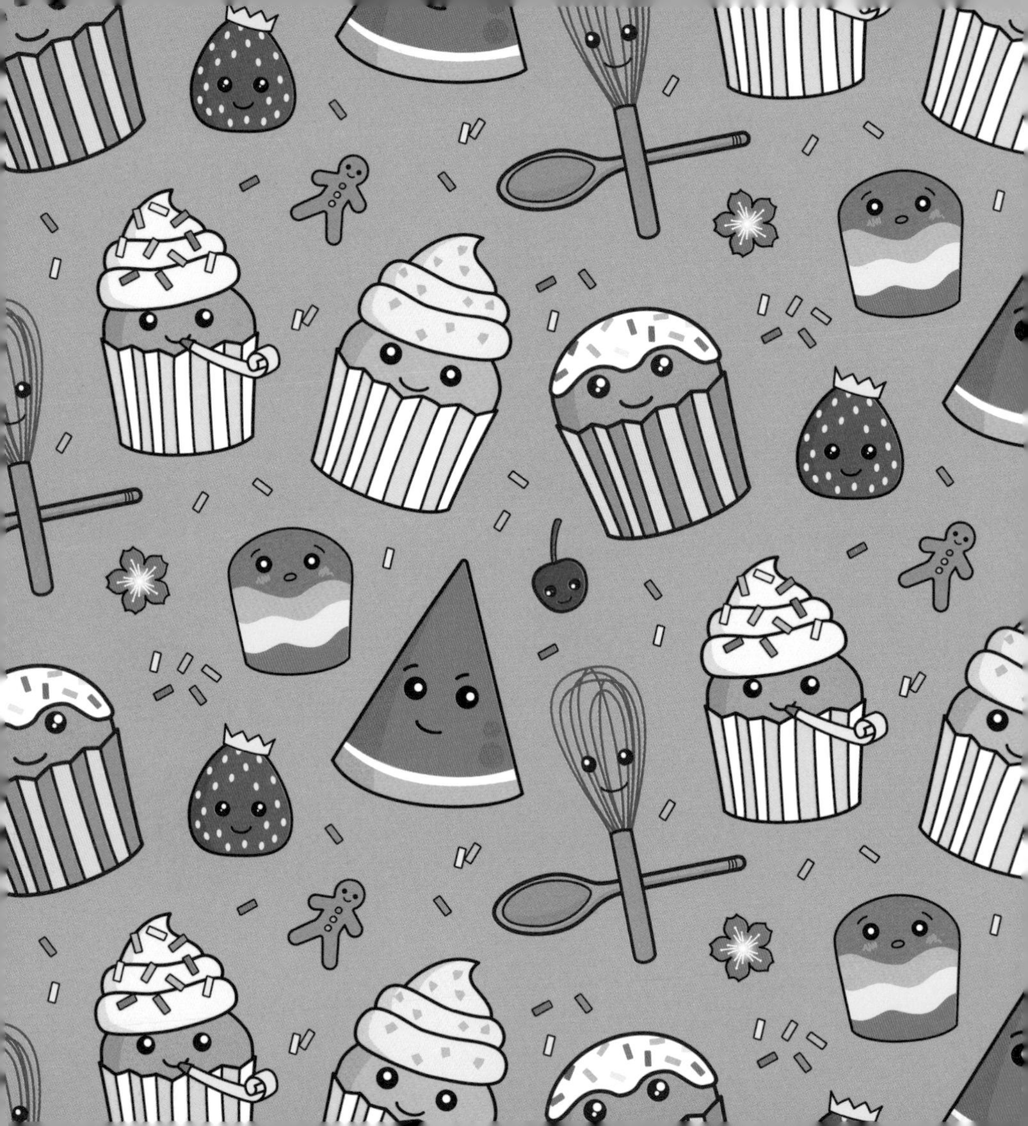